A Guide for Using

Hoot

in the Classroom

Based on the novel written by Carl Hiaasen

This guide written by

Melissa Hart, M.F.A.

Teacher Created Resources, Inc.
6421 Industry Way
Westminster, CA 92683
www.teachercreated.com
©*2006 Teacher Created Resources, Inc.*
Made in U.S.A.
ISBN-1-4206-2587-X

Edited by
Heather Douglas

Illustrated by
Kevin McCarthy

Cover Art by
Courtney Barnes

Table of Contents

Introduction

A good book can enrich our lives like a good friend. Fictional characters can inspire us and teach us about the world in which we live. We may turn to books for companionship, entertainment, and guidance. A truly beloved book may touch our lives forever.

Great care has been taken with Literature Units to select books that are sure to become your students' good friends!

Teachers who use this unit will find the following features to supplement their own ideas:

- Sample Lesson Plans

- Pre-Reading Activities

- A Biographical Sketch and Picture of the Author

- A Book Summary

- Vocabulary Lists and Suggested Vocabulary Activities

- Chapters grouped for study with each section including:

  — *quizzes*

  — *hands-on projects*

  — *cooperative learning activities*

  — *cross-curricular connections*

  — *extensions into the reader's life*

- Post-Reading Activities

- Book Report Ideas

- Research Activities

- Culminating Activities

- Three Different Options for Unit Tests

- Bibliography

- Answer Key

We are certain this unit will be a valuable addition to your own curriculum ideas to supplement *Hoot*.

Sample Lesson Plans

The time it takes to complete the suggested lessons below will vary, depending on the type of activity, your students' abilities, and their interest levels.

Lesson 1
- Introduce and complete some or all of the pre-reading activities from "Before Reading the Book." (page 5)
- Read "About the Author" with students. (page 6)
- Introduce the vocabulary list for Section 1. (page 8)

Lesson 2
- Read Chapters 1–5. As you read, discuss vocabulary words, using the book context to explain their meanings.
- Locate Coconut Cove, Florida on a classroom map. *Hoot* takes place in Coconut Cove.
- Choose vocabulary activities to complete. (page 9)
- Make a papier-mâchè owl. (page 11)
- Learn to deal with bullies. (page 12)
- Learn about Florida. (page 13)
- Describe your hometown. (page 14)
- Administer the Section 1 Quiz. (page 10)
- Introduce the vocabulary list for Section 2. (page 8)

Lesson 3
- Read Chapters 6–9. Discuss vocabulary words.
- Choose a vocabulary activity to complete. (page 9)
- Make insect cookies. (page 16)
- Give shoebox gifts. (page 17)
- Investigate electrical storms. (page 18)
- Discover the power of persistence. (page 19)
- Administer the Section 2 Quiz. (page 15)
- Introduce the vocabulary list for Section 3. (page 8)

Lesson 4
- Read Chapters 10–14. Discuss vocabulary words.
- Choose a vocabulary activity to complete. (page 9)
- Learn to administer first aid. (page 21)
- Learn all about raptors. (page 22)

- Write a business letter. (page 23)
- Examine what's right and what's wrong. (page 24)
- Administer the Section 3 Quiz. (page 20)
- Introduce the vocabulary list for Section 4. (page 8)

Lesson 5
- Read Chapters 15–17. Discuss vocabulary words.
- Choose a vocabulary activity to complete. (page 9)
- Create a diorama of the Everglades. (page 26)
- Film a commercial. (page 27)
- Learn about the Seminole Indians. (page 28)
- Create a creative protest. (page 29)
- Administer the Section 4 Quiz. (page 25)
- Introduce the vocabulary list for Section 5. (page 8)

Lesson 6
- Read Chapters 18–Epilogue. Discuss vocabulary words.
- Choose a vocabulary activity to complete. (page 9)
- Make a newspaper. (page 31)
- Build a wildlife habitat. (page 32)
- Explore current events. (page 33)
- Make a difference in the world. (page 34)
- Administer the Section 5 Quiz. (page 30)

Lesson 7
- Discuss questions students have about the book. (page 35)
- Assign a book report and research activity. (pages 36–37)
- Begin work on one or more culminating activities. (pages 38–42)

Lesson 8
- Choose and administer one or more of the Unit Tests. (pages 43–45)
- Discuss students' feelings about the book.
- Provide a bibliography of related reading. (page 46)

Before Reading the Book

Before you begin reading *Hoot* with your students, complete one or more of the following pre-reading activities to stimulate their interest and enhance their comprehension.

1. Examine the cover of the book. Ask students to predict the book's plot, characters, and setting. Ask them if they think the book is humorous or serious.

2. Discuss the title. Ask students what type of birds "hoot," and see if they can predict anything about the book from its title.

3. Answer these questions:

   - What would it feel like to be the new kid in town?

   - Why might someone commit an act of vandalism?

   - How might you approach someone who is being a bully?

   - What would it feel like to solve a mystery?

   - Why might someone trespass on private property?

   - Have you ever fought for something you believe in?

   - What might inspire a person to challenge authority?

   - How can people balance urban growth with wildlife preservation?

4. Direct students to work in groups to brainstorm how they might go about protecting the environment.

5. Direct students to work in groups to list ways to protest against a decision or event in a peaceful manner. You may want to describe the pacifist methods used by Gandhi and Dr. Martin Luther King, Jr.

6. Brainstorm ways in which a young person can help to change the world for the better. Often, children feel that they have no control. However, simply by offering a smile or voicing an opinion, young people may make a difference in the world.

7. Work in groups to discuss why it might be important to protect the environment. Examine the connection between plants, animals, and people. Discuss the food chain and how raptors—and owls in particular—fit into it. Explore the importance of keeping land wild and undeveloped for wildlife.

About the Author

Carl Hiaasen was born on March 12, 1953 in Plantation, Florida. He was the first of four children. His father presented him with a typewriter when he was six years old. As a young person, Carl wrote stories about neighborhood kickball and softball games and gave them away to his friends.

Carl read constantly as a child. In fourth grade, he loved the Hardy Boys series. J.D. Salinger was a favorite author. He also enjoyed the sports biographies of Lou Gehrig and Vince Lombardi.

He graduated from the University of Florida with a degree in journalism. At age 23, he began to write for Florida's largest newspaper, *The Miami Herald*. Much of his writing concentrated on construction and property development. His stories often exposed developers' plans to destroy the natural beauty of Florida.

In the 1980s, Carl began to write novels. His books have been published in 30 languages! Many people refer to his novels as "environmental thrillers." His books are often mysterious crime thrillers, full of humor and strange characters.

Carl decided to write *Hoot* because of the continuing controversy surrounding the habitat of burrowing owls in Florida. He also notes that his fifth grade stepson and his nephew and niece wanted to read what he'd written, and he wanted to provide them with a book for children. Writing *Hoot* didn't take very long because Carl enjoyed it so much. He relied on memories of his own childhood for parts of *Hoot*. The book won the Newbery Honor Award in 2003.

Carl almost always writes about issues affecting Florida. He finds this area full of weird, true-life events which inspire his fiction. These days, he lives in the Florida Keys and has pet snakes. He's also recorded two songs with songwriter Warren Zevon!

Carl writes a weekly column for *The Miami Herald*. His newest novel for children is titled *Flush*, about a boy who investigates the environmental destruction caused by a casino boat in Florida. He says of his work, "I would like my children and grandchildren to be able to grow up in a place where they can always see a bald eagle or a manatee or a school of dolphins—or a pair of little burrowing owls, for that matter."

Hoot

by Carl Hiaasen

(Knopf, 2002)

Roy Eberhardt spots a barefoot boy running alongside the school bus in his new town of Coconut Cove. He doesn't get a chance to find out where the boy is going, however, because a local bully tries to beat him up.

Meanwhile, Officer Delinko is sent to the construction site of the future Mother Paula's Pancake House to investigate reports of vandalism. Someone has been pulling up survey stakes on the site and putting alligators in the port-a-potties.

Roy decides to investigate the mystery of the barefoot boy. In attempting to find him, he becomes friends with Beatrice Leep—a tough-talking girl at his middle school. Beatrice introduces him to her brother, nicknamed Mullet Fingers.

Mullet Fingers is concerned about the Mother Paula's construction site. Roy investigates the land for himself and discovers that it is home to burrowing owls that live in the ground. Construction on the site would destroy their home.

Officer Delinko is also worried about trouble at the construction site. His patrol car is vandalized while he is on the property, and then someone lets loose poisonous snakes that threaten the site's guard dogs.

Mullet Fingers is injured as he tries to save the burrowing owls. Roy lies in order to help him. Roy's parents grow concerned, and they tell him that he needs to think long and hard about what is worth fighting for.

Roy decides to fight for the burrowing owls. Rather than vandalize private property, however, he goes about his investigation by examining official building documents. He discovers that a mandatory building document is missing. This inspires him to give Mullet Fingers his mother's digital camera in order to prove the presence of the owls.

Mother Paula's holds a groundbreaking ceremony. In the midst of it, Roy and Mullet Fingers and Beatrice stage their own protest. Just when it looks like the little owls are doomed, unexpected help arrives. Will they be saved after all?

Vocabulary Lists

Below are lists of vocabulary words and idiomatic phrases for each section of chapters. The following page offers ideas for using this vocabulary in classroom activities.

Section 1 (Chapters 1–5)

ambush(ed)	snide(ly)
vandalism	baleful(ly)
monetary	provoke
humidity	sinewy
skeptical	gore(d)
dogged(ly)	disgruntled
sarcasm	dispatcher
menace	forthright(ly)
consternation	civilized

Section 2 (Chapters 6–9)

assertive	homicide
surveillance	fervent(ly)
perpetrator(s)	informant
jeopardy	noncommittal
altercation	queasy
ominous(ly)	incentive
sodden	scabrous
menacing(ly)	nonchalant(ly)
caustic(ly)	travesty

Section 3 (Chapters 10–14)

truss(ed)	fugitive	rebuke
beaker	subterranean	emblem
recurring	commode	reconnaissance
ballistic	terse(ly)	salvage
exasperate(d)	interrogating	dilapidated
cowling	turbulence	derelict

Section 4 (Chapters 15–17)

amateur	morph(ed)	hoodlum
vile	castanets	rankle(d)
malevolent(ly)	sullen	bungle(d)
patronizing	bogus	heist
fiasco	harrowing	vault(ed)
cheesy	rap sheet	agitate(d)

Section 5 (Chapters 18–Epilogue)

involuntary	improbable	withering
frenzied	crackerjack	mutilate(d)
extravaganza	charitable	flamboyant
jurisdiction	dignitaries	toupee
lustrous	slanderous	melodramatic
allegation	impertinent	tarpon

8

Vocabulary Activities

You can help your students learn the vocabulary words in *Hoot* by providing them with the stimulating vocabulary activities below.

1. Ask students to work in groups to create an **Illustrated Book** of the vocabulary words and their meanings.

2. Separate students into groups. Direct groups to use vocabulary words to create **Crossword Puzzles** and **Word Searches**. Groups can trade puzzles with each other and complete them, then check each other's work.

3. Play **Guess the Definition**. One student writes down the correct definition of the vocabulary word. The others write down false definitions, close enough to the original definition that their classmates might be fooled. Read all definitions, and then challenge students to guess the correct one. The students whose definitions mislead their classmates get a point for each student fooled.

4. Use the word in five different sentences. Compare sentences and discuss.

5. Write a **Short Story** using as many of the words as possible. Students may then read their stories in groups.

6. Encourage your students to use each new vocabulary word in a conversation five times during one day. They can take notes on how and when the word was used and then share their experience with the class.

7. Play **Vocabulary Charades**. Each student or group of students gets a word to act out. Other students must guess the word.

8. Play **Vocabulary Pictures**. Each student or group of students must draw a picture representing a word on the chalkboard or on paper. Other students must guess the word.

9. Challenge students to a **Vocabulary Bee**. In groups or separately, students must spell the word correctly, and give its proper definition.

10. Talk about **Parts of Speech** by discussing the different forms that a word may take. For instance, some words may function as nouns, as well as verbs. The word "gore" is a good example of a word which can be both a noun and a verb. Some words which look alike may have completely different meanings; in *Hoot*, the word "constellation" is used to describe a particular formation of stars, but it may also be used to describe a group of people or objects.

11. Ask your students to make **Flash Cards** with the word printed on one side and the definition printed on the other. Ask your students to work with a younger class to help them learn the definitions of the new words, using the flash cards.

12. Create **Word Art** by writing the words with glue on stiff paper, and then covering the glue with glitter or sand. Alternatively, students may write the words with a squeeze bottle full of jam on bread to create an edible lesson!

Quiz Time

Answer the following questions about Chapters 1–5.

1. For what reasons is Roy so interested in the strange boy outside the bus window?

   _____

   _____

2. Why doesn't Roy have a hometown? _____

   _____

   _____

3. Why does Miss Hennepin suspend Roy from the bus?_____

   _____

   _____

4. How does Mr. Eberhardt react when he finds out about Roy's fight with Dana?

   _____

   _____

5. For what reason does Officer Delinko think that someone put alligators in the toilets?

   _____

   _____

6. Why does Officer Delinko want to solve the mystery of the vandalism at the construction site?

   _____

   _____

7. Why is Beatrice surprised when Roy talks to her in the cafeteria? _____

   _____

   _____

8. What does Roy find in the thicket near the golf course? _____

   _____

Papier-Mâchè Owl

While patrolling the construction site, Officer Delinko sees a pair of burrowing owls. He sees that they are only eight or nine inches tall, with spotted wings and amber eyes. You can make a life-sized papier-mâchè burrowing owl using just a few simple items.

Materials

- small balloons

- eight-or nine-inch long strips of newspaper

- tempera paint—brown, white, and black

- flour

- water

Directions

1. First, research burrowing owls on the Internet or in a book or encyclopedia. Note their colors and markings. Make a simple sketch of a burrowing owl on a piece of paper to guide you in creating your papier-mâchè owl.

2. Now, tear newspaper into strips, about 1" by 8" (about 2.5 cm x 20 cm). Then, make a paste using 1/2 cup (125 ml) flour and 1/2 cup (125 ml) water. The paste should look thick and creamy. Add more flour or water as needed.

3. Blow up your balloon and tie it closed. Dip each strip of newspaper into the paste so that it is covered, and then stick it to your balloon. Continue this until your balloon is covered with strips of newspaper.

4. Let your balloon dry overnight. If you'd like a sturdier sculpture, add one more layer of newspaper strips dipped in paste the next day. It is important to let it dry completely.

5. Now, paint your papier-mâchè balloon to look like a burrowing owl. Remember that the knot of the balloon is above your owl's head. When the paint is dry, tie a string around the knot of your balloon and hang it from the ceiling.

Dealing with Bullies

Roy is attacked on the bus by Dana Matherson, who is older and bigger than he. Usually, he tolerates Dana's bullying. However, on the day that Dana tries to choke him, Roy finds himself fighting back. This gets him in trouble with the vice-principal at school.

Bullying is a serious problem in many schools. Think about the ways in which it might be addressed and stopped.

First, divide into four groups. Each group should choose a question from the list below. Write down possible answers to your question on your own sheet of paper. Then, share your answers with your group and brainstorm other possible solutions for ten minutes. When you are finished, share all answers with the rest of your class. Ask if they have any suggestions to answer your group's question as well.

Group 1
Question: What motivates bullies to pick on people? _____

_____

_____

_____

Group 2
Question: What actions might the victim of a bully take to protect him or herself? _____

_____

_____

_____

Group 3
Question: What actions should teachers and schools take to prevent bullying? _____

_____

_____

_____

Group 4
Question: What actions should parents take to prevent bullying? _____

_____

_____

_____

All About Florida!

Roy's family moves a great deal. This time, they end up in Florida. What do you know about Florida? Use encyclopedias, books, magazines, or the Internet to answer the questions below.

1. When did Florida become part of the United States?

   _____

2. How large is Florida in square miles or kilometers? _____

3. Name three types of native mammals that live in Florida:

   a. _____

   b. _____

   c. _____

4. Name three types of native reptiles that live in Florida:

   a. _____

   b. _____

   c. _____

5. Name three types of native birds that live in Florida:

   a. _____

   b. _____

   c. _____

6. Describe the Everglades in a few sentences below:

   _____

   _____

   _____

7. What is Florida's state bird?

   _____

8. What is Florida's state tree?

   _____

9. What is Florida's state flower?

   _____

10. You may wish to draw a picture of Florida on the back of this page. Name the ocean that surrounds it.

    _____

Description

The author of *Hoot*, Carl Hiaasen, describes Roy's new town of Coconut Cove with vivid details about the flora and fauna that live in Florida. Good descriptive writing makes the reader imagine what it is like to be in the same setting with a book's narrator. It appeals to all five senses, with details about the sounds, smells, and sights in a place, as well as what one might taste and feel there.

Below, write a descriptive paragraph about your own city. In your writing, make sure to appeal to the reader's five senses. Help your reader to imagine what it would be like to live in your city. Your paragraph should be 5–7 sentences long.

_____

_____

_____

_____

_____

_____

_____

Now, describe your favorite place in one paragraph. It may be indoors or outdoors, in your city, or in another one far away. Write down as many sensory details as possible to show readers why you like this setting most of all.

_____

_____

_____

_____

_____

_____

_____

Quiz Time

Answer the following questions about Chapters 6–9.

1. Why does Officer Delinko have to go on desk duty?

   _____

   _____

2. Why does Beatrice take Roy's bike?

   _____

   _____

3. For what purpose does Beatrice bite a hole in Roy's bike tire?

   _____

   _____

4. Why is Roy allowed back on the school bus?

   _____

   _____

5. Why does Roy let Dana hit him on the school bus?

   _____

   _____

6. For what reasons does Roy try not to worry his parents?

   _____

   _____

7. Why does Kalo take his dogs away from the construction site?

   _____

   _____

8. Why is Curly in trouble with Chuck Muckle?

   _____

   _____

Insect Cookies

Note to Teacher: Send home a written note with students, inquiring about pertinent food allergies, well in advance of preparing these cookies.

Burrowing owls eat insects such as beetles, crickets, and grasshoppers. You probably don't want to eat an insect, but you can make sugar cookies in the shape of insects enjoyed by the burrowing owls!

This recipe makes 36 cookies.

Ingredients

- 1/3 cup (about 80 ml) butter or margarine, softened
- 1/3 cup (about 80 ml) shortening
- 3/4 cup (about 180 ml) sugar
- 1 teaspoon baking powder
- a pinch of salt
- 1 egg
- 1 teaspoon vanilla
- 2 cups (about 1/2 liter) all-purpose flour
- cookie decorations, if desired

Materials

- cardboard
- pencil
- scissors
- oven
- two bowls
- rolling pin
- electric mixer
- butter knife
- baking sheets
- spatula
- cooling rack

Directions

1. First, draw 4" (about 10 cm) insect shapes on cardboard. Cut the shapes out with scissors. Set aside.

2. Now, beat butter and shortening with an electric mixer or pastry cutter. Add sugar, baking powder, and a pinch of salt. Mix until well combined. Beat in egg and vanilla. Then, beat in flour.

3. Cover and chill the dough for at least an hour.

4. Preheat the oven to 375° F (190°C). Split the dough in half. Put one half back in the refrigerator. Roll out the other half on a well-floured surface. Place your cardboard shapes on the dough. Cut around them with a butter knife.

5. Carefully lift each shape onto an ungreased baking sheet with a floured spatula. Decorate cookies, if desired.

6. Bake for 7 to 8 minutes, until edges are firm and bottoms are lightly browned. Then, roll out the other half of your dough, cut shapes, and bake.

Shoebox Gifts

Roy wants to help the barefoot boy, so he tries to bring him a pair of shoes in a shoebox. Later, he hears that the boy is Beatrice's brother and is homeless.

Many charitable organizations fill shoeboxes full of useful items to give to homeless or sick children. Why not start such a tradition in your own community?

First, locate a local organization that will accept donations for homeless or sick children. With an adult's help, contact a shelter or children's wing of a hospital.

Now, organize students into six groups. Each group will fill a shoebox with cards and other items that might help a disadvantaged child. First, decorate your shoebox with colored paper, pens, glitter, sequins, and anything else that will make it a work of art.

Here are some items to consider as you fill your shoebox.

- handmade greeting cards

- collages

- colorful stickers

- felt or paper bookmarkers

- origami animals

- a special pen or pencil

- a pad of paper, each page accented with stickers

- a pack of crayons or pens

- a picture frame decorated with glued-on buttons or sequins

- a tape or CD of your favorite music

- a hand-beaded key chain or necklace

- homemade clay in a plastic bag

- insect cookies from page 16

When you have finished assembling your shoebox, make a gift tag and ask all of the people in your group to sign their first name. Then, deliver your gifts and know that you have brightened another child's day!

Electrical Storm!

Roy finds himself stranded without his bicycle in an electrical storm. Such storms happen frequently in Florida, where Roy lives.

How is an electrical storm caused? During a storm, friction from dust, ice, and water droplets blown about by quickly-moving air causes an accumulation of positive electrical charges within a storm cloud. This positive charge causes friction when it meets the negatively-charged ground. This huge difference in charges creates a great deal of pressure. This static electricity is responsible for lightning.

Conduct the following four experiments to see for yourself how the build-up of electrons on each object creates static electricity.

Materials

- ground pepper
- plastic comb
- wool or faux fur
- metal doorknob

- bowl of puffed rice
- two rubber balloons

Directions

1. First, sprinkle pepper on the top of a table or desk. Quickly rub a comb with the wool or faux fur—this will produce a negative charge. Now, hold the comb an inch over the pepper to see what happens!

2. Next, turn off all the lights in the room so that it is quite dark. Vigorously rub the comb again with a piece of wool or fur. Hold the comb near a metal doorknob to see what happens!

3. Now, blow up two balloons and tie them closed. Rub each of them on your sleeve. Darken the room, then rub the two balloons together to see what happens!

4. Finally, choose one student to run the comb through his/her hair. Place the comb in the bowl of dry puffed rice and see what happens!

The Power of Persistence

Roy is a persistent young man; that is, he wants to find out the mystery behind the barefoot boy, and he braves bullies and electrical storms to do so. Thanks to his determination, in Chapter 7 he finds out more about Mullet Fingers than he ever imagined.

Think about a time that you showed the power of persistence. Perhaps you kept practicing a skill like basketball or singing until you were finally proficient. Maybe you believed in something strongly—like rescuing a homeless animal or riding your bike to the park—and you stood up for your cause until you were successful. Or perhaps, thanks to your persistent investigation, you solved a mystery of your own.

Below, fill out the chart to show how your persistence paid off.

My Goal	
Steps I Took to Achieve It	
The Outcome	

Quiz Time

Answer the following questions about Chapters 10–14.

1. How does Beatrice punish Dana for attacking Roy in the closet?

_____

_____

2. Why doesn't Lonna try to find her son?

_____

_____

3. How does Mullet Fingers get bitten?

_____

_____

4. Why does Roy give the emergency room clerk his own name instead of that of Mullet Fingers?

_____

_____

5. Why is Mullet Fingers concerned about the burrowing owls?

_____

_____

6. Why does Roy go to see Dana Matherson?

_____

_____

7. How did Chuck E. Muckle respond when he received Beatrice's letter?

_____

_____

8. What does Mullet Fingers show Roy when he takes him to the creek?

_____

_____

First Aid

Roy knows how to treat the puncture wounds on Mullet Finger's arm because he's taken a first-aid course. Knowing how to bandage cuts and treat sprains is extremely useful. Choose a partner and practice the techniques below.

Note to teacher: For extra kid-appeal, you may choose to purchase fake blood, often available at drug stores and party supply stores in the fall. Other materials you will need are soap and water, latex gloves, sterile dressings, athletic tape, scissors, washcloths, gauze, icepacks or water frozen in paper cups, and elastic bandages.

Cuts and Puncture Wounds

1. Wash your hands. Clean the cut or puncture wound with soap and warm water. Carefully wash away any dirt.

2. With a washcloth, apply direct pressure to the wound until the bleeding stops.

3. Cut a piece of dressing so that it extends ½" (1.3 cm) beyond the wound. Place dressing on top of wound.

4. Cut four strips of athletic tape and affix them to the dressing and skin on all four sides of the dressing, making sure the bandage is not too tight or too loose.

   Important Note: Take the injured person to the doctor if the wound is deep, if it won't stop bleeding, or if a fever is present.

Insect Sting

1. Make sure the injured person isn't having an allergic reaction. If swelling spreads to the face or neck, or the person begins to wheeze or feel dizzy, get professional medical help immediately.

2. If there is no allergic reaction, wash your hands, and then wash the location of the sting with soap and water.

3. Remove the stinger by wiping a 4" x 4" (10 cm x 10 cm) piece of gauze over the area, or by scraping the area gently with a piece of stiff paper.

4. Apply ice for ten minutes to reduce swelling.

Muscle Strains

1. Help the injured person to a dry, warm location.

2. Wash your hands, then rub ice on the injured area for five to ten minutes.

3. Wrap an elastic bandage around the injured area to reduce swelling. If you don't have an elastic bandage, wrap a piece of clothing such as a sock or shirt around the injured area.

4. Elevate the injured area above the heart. Prop an injured leg on a table, or on books stacked on a chair. If an arm is injured, ask the person to rest his or her hand on her head, keeping the arm above heart-level.

All About Raptors!

Roy discovers many different types of raptors in *Hoot*. A raptor is a bird of prey. It hunts using its talons, and tears its prey apart with its beak.

In groups of three, choose a species of raptor from the list below.

Raptor List

- burrowing owl
- great-horned owl
- osprey
- red-tailed hawk
- peregrine falcon
- American kestrel
- bald eagle
- golden eagle
- Swainson's hawk
- spotted owl
- northern goshawk
- snowy owl

Using the Internet, books and encyclopedias, research your chosen raptor and fill out the form below. Then, give a report on your raptor for the rest of the class. You may want to show pictures and video clips to give people a better understanding of your bird of prey.

Raptor Report

Name of Raptor: _____

Average Height: _____

Average Weight: _____

Average Wingspan: _____

Color and Markings:_____

Territory: _____

Favorite Foods: _____

Hunting Technique: _____

Threats to their safety: _____

Any other special characteristics:_____

_____

_____

_____

Writing a Business Letter

Mullet Fingers asks Beatrice to write a letter to Mother Paula's Pancake House, expressing concern about the burrowing owls that live on the construction site. People write business letters for a variety of reasons—to express concern about a topic, as Beatrice does, or to give thanks for something in particular that the business or individual has done.

A business letter should be formal and polite, following the format below. It may be typed or written neatly on nice stationery. Use the form below to write a rough draft of a business letter. You may want to write to a favorite restaurant, or to your city mayor, or to the head of your local parks and recreation department. The choice is yours!

When you have finished your rough draft, type or neatly copy your letter onto stationery. Find the appropriate address in your phone book or on the Internet, address an envelope, stamp it, and mail your letter.

Business Letter
Rough Draft

_____

_____
(Your Address)

_____
(Today's Date)

_____
(Name of Business Owner)

_____

_____
(Address of Business)

Dear Mr./Ms._____:

_____

_____

_____

_____

_____

_____

_____

(Body of your letter; can be one or two paragraphs)

Sincerely,

_____
(Your Name)

What's Right and What's Wrong

> Sometimes you're going to be faced with situations where the line isn't clear between what's right and what's wrong. Your heart will tell you to do one thing, and your brain will tell you to do something different. In the end, all that's left is to look at both sides and go with your best judgment.
>
> —*Hoot* by Carl Hiaasen

Roy's mother gives him the advice above after she learns about the plight of the burrowing owls. Think about a time you had a problem and your heart told you one thing while your head told you another. Fill out the chart below to show how you solved your conflict.

Description of My Problem: _____

_____

_____

_____

What My Heart Said:	What My Brain Said:
Analysis of Side One:	**Analysis of Side Two:**

How I Solved the Problem: _____

_____

_____

_____

Quiz Time

Answer the following questions about Chapters 15–17.

1. Why does Roy tell Dana about a carton of cigarettes in the construction trailer?

   _____

   _____

2. Why might the police lock Dana up in juvenile hall?

   _____

   _____

3. Why did someone remove the seats on the construction equipment at the Mother Paula's site?

   _____

   _____

4. What does Roy discover on the airboat trip through the Everglades?

   _____

   _____

5. Why does Beatrice break into Roy's house?

   _____

   _____

6. Why does Chuck Muckle ask Curly to say that the owl burrows are deserted?

   _____

   _____

7. What does Officer Delinko discover when he gives Dana a plastic alligator?

   _____

   _____

8. For what reason might the folder with permits and inspection notices for Mother Paula's Pancake House be checked out?

   _____

   _____

Everglades Diorama

Roy's family takes a trip through the Everglades on an airboat. He realizes then that there are wild places in Florida, just as there were in Montana. Even if you've never seen the Everglades, you can make a diorama to give you a sense of this unique wilderness.

A diorama is a three-dimensional life-sized scene in which objects are arranged against a decorated background. Reread Roy's description of his visit to the Everglades and create a diorama based on what he observes.

Materials

- shoebox
- scratch paper for design
- colored paper
- scissors
- books and/or the Internet

- glue
- plastic animals such eagles, snakes, raccoons, turtles, etc. (optional)
- pens and/or crayons and/or paint
- sequins, beads, glitter, and other decorative objects

Directions

1. First, remove the lid and place your shoebox on one side. You will create your diorama inside the box. It may be vertical or horizontal.

2. Now, sketch your diorama on scratch paper. Think about how you'll depict the Everglades. Will you hang birds from the top of your diorama? Will you create water full of turtles and alligators? How will you create trees and other plant life? Consult books and the Internet for further examples of what the Everglades look like.

3. Finally, create your diorama. Make sure to include the wildlife that Roy describes in *Hoot*. You may want to glue blue-colored paper to the top and sides of your diorama for a sky, or to the bottom to depict water. Use three-dimensional cut-outs with stands, such as the ones below, to add interest and excitement to your artwork!

Film a Commercial!

Kimberly Lou Dixon is the actress who portrays Mother Paula in the commercials for the pancake house. She promotes the weekend special—endless pancakes, plus sausage and coffee, all for $6.95.

There are numerous advertising techniques. Mother Paula's uses a "Plain Folks" technique with the promise of good value and good food. Here is a brief list of other advertising techniques:

- **Bandwagon:** Suggests that everyone is using a particular product, and you should use it, too.

- **Facts and Figures:** Statistical information and testimonials from experts to prove that you should use a product.

- **Fear:** Suggests that if you use this product, you'll be protected against something or someone.

- **Plain Folks:** Suggests that the product is practical and good for everyday people.

- **Testimonial:** A famous person endorses the product.

- **Warm and Fuzzy:** Uses adorable and loving images of children and animals to sell a product.

- **Wit and Humor:** Uses a funny story to entice people to buy a product.

Now, it's your turn to film a 30-second commercial. Borrow a video camera from school or from a parent, or rent one at a local rental store.

Break into groups of four. Decide what product or service you will sell. Plan your commercial in the space below. Decide who will write your commercial, who will act in it, and who will film it. When you are finished, make popcorn and watch each commercial as a class!

Commercial Plan

Name of product or service to be sold: _____

Why should people buy this product or service? _____

_____

What advertising techniques will you use so that people will buy your product or service?

_____

Who will write your commercial? _____

Who will act in your commercial? _____

Who will film your commercial? _____

Will you need costumes, props, and other items? _____

_____

The Seminole Indians

The Seminole Indians live in Florida, and Roy tricks Dana into thinking he's purchased a carton of cigarettes from their reservation.

What do you know about the Seminole Indians? Using books, encyclopedias, and the Internet, answer the questions below.

1. In what year did the Seminole nation come into existence, and which groups made up this nation?

   _____

   _____

2. Why did the United States government want to remove the Seminole Indians from Florida?

   _____

   _____

3. Who is Seminole leader Osceola, and why is he famous?

   _____

   _____

4. Why do the Seminoles call themselves "The Unconquered People"?

   _____

   _____

5. What type of artwork do the Seminoles produce?

   _____

   _____

6. How many reservations does the Seminole tribe maintain in Florida, and what are their names?

   _____

   _____

7. What two types of language do the Seminoles speak, aside from English?

   _____

   _____

8. What is Seminole patchwork?

   _____

   _____

9. What is the Seminole "Chickee"? _____

   Draw a picture of it on the back of this page.

Creative Protests

Mullet Fingers finds creative ways to protest the building of a Mother Paula's Pancake House over the burrowing owls' homes. Roy also begins to discover interesting ways to challenge injustice. Below, examine each boy's actions. Then, write the reasons for these actions.

Mullet Fingers		Roy Eberhardt	
Action	**Reason**	**Action**	**Reason**
Pulls out all the survey stakes at the construction site		Gives his own name to the emergency room staff.	
Puts alligators in the port-a-potties		Tells Dana Matherson about a carton of cigarettes at the construction site	
Paints the windows of the patrol car black		Goes to City Hall to find the file for Mother Paula's Pancake House	
Puts snakes in with the guard dogs		Feeds crickets to the burrowing owls	
Removes seats from bulldozers		Gave current events report on burrowing owls	

Mullet Fingers puts himself in danger with his protests. Roy goes about his protest in a less-harmful manner. Think about something you believe in strongly. How might you protest creatively, without breaking the law or harming anyone? Write your answer on the back of this paper.

Quiz Time

Answer the following questions about Chapters 18–Epilogue.

1. How does Officer Delinko feel when he discovers the burrowing owls living on the construction site?

   _____

   _____

2. Why does Roy borrow his mother's camera?

   _____

   _____

3. Why does Mullet Fingers push Roy out of the truck?

   _____

   _____

4. How is Roy's report in class related to "Current Events"?

   _____

   _____

5. How does Kimberly Lou Dixon react when she learns about the owls?

   _____

   _____

6. Why doesn't Officer Delinko tell Chuck Muckle that Mullet Fingers's snakes are only rubber?

   _____

   _____

7. Why is the missing Environmental Impact Statement so important in the case against Mother Paula's?

   _____

   _____

8. Where do you think Mullet Fingers is living now, and why?

   _____

   _____

In the News

Roy gives the file on Mother Paula's Pancake House to a reporter from the *Gazette*. A story about the missing Environmental Impact Statement halts the building project completely.

Form groups of four. Study your local newspaper.

Then, using what you know about the controversy surrounding the burrowing owl issue, design and write a 2–3 page newspaper. Assign each person in your group an article to write. Make sure to have articles related to the groundbreaking ceremony, the people involved, and the lack of the Environmental Impact Statement.

Your newspaper should include the following:

- A name
- A date
- A masthead with the editor's name and contact information

- Several articles with interviews
- Photographs
- Print ads
- Classified ads

Build a Wildlife Habitat

Mullet Fingers, along with Roy and Beatrice, preserves the burrowing owls' habitat. Your class can create its very own habitat for birds and other wildlife at your school. Consider adopting a piece of land on or around your school and dedicate it to the wildlife in your area.

Using the suggestions below, offer a combination of food, water, shelter and space to attract birds, butterflies, insects and small mammals.

Birds

Different species of birds enjoy various types of food in feeders. Some birds prefer feeders that hang from branches or metal stands. Other birds like to eat off the ground. Sunflower seeds appeal to some birds, while others love blocks of suet hung from branches. Birds such as robins and mockingbirds adore citrus, chopped apples, bananas, and raisins. Don't forget to place a shallow dish of water in your habitat for use as a bird bath!

Butterflies

Butterflies get nectar from flowers. Different types of butterflies enjoy different types of flowering plants. They especially like Buddleia, or butterfly bush. Find out what species of butterflies are common in your area, and plant the flowering bushes they prefer. Nectar feeders also attract butterflies. Provide a light-colored rock or concrete garden sculpture on which butterflies may bask in the sun. Include a shallow dish of water, or water in the depression of a rock, so that butterflies will have something to drink as well.

Reptiles and Amphibians

Most toads, frogs, lizards, turtles, and snakes are harmless, beneficial creatures who feed on destructive insects and rodents. You can easily provide shelter for reptiles and amphibians. A pile of rocks in a sunny spot offers a place to bask in the sun. Shade-tolerant groundcovers under trees provide cool shelter, as does a thick layer of leaves piled on the ground. Reptiles and amphibians also enjoy stumps, logs and rock piles, as well as shallow bowls of water.

Backyard Habitat Programs

The National Wildlife Federation (NWF) sponsors a certification program designed to help people plan and create a wildlife habitat plan. NWF will send your class an application package and instructions. For more information, write to:

Backyard Wildlife Habitat Program
National Wildlife Federation
8925 Leesburg Pike
Vienna, VA 22184-0001

What's Up?

Mr. Ryan, Roy's history teacher, asks students to bring in a topic for a current events discussion each Tuesday. Roy begins a discussion about Mother Paula's groundbreaking ceremony, which inspires his classmates to come out and protest the construction.

You can hold a similar classroom discussion. Using newspapers and weekly magazines such as *Newsweek*, *Time*, and *U.S. News*, research a current event of your choosing. Prepare for your discussion by filling out the form below.

Current Event

1. Describe your current event: _____

   _____

2. Who are the people involved in this event? _____

   _____

3. Where is this event taking place? _____

   _____

4. When did this event take place? Is it still occurring? _____

   _____

5. How might this event impact your area? _____

   _____

   _____

6. How might this event affect your classmates and teacher? _____

   _____

   _____

7. What specific actions can you take regarding this event?_____

   _____

   _____

   _____

Now, present your current event in front of your class. Make sure to explain the answers to each of the questions above.

Finally, ask the class to brainstorm possible answers to questions 5 through 7. Write their answers on the board.

Making a Difference

Roy does many good deeds throughout the book which help his friends, his family, and the burrowing owls. For instance, he allows Beatrice to stay at his house when her family is being mean, and he helps to save the owls from destruction. He even brings Mullet Fingers a pair of sneakers.

In turn, other people help Roy. Beatrice defends him from Dana Matherson. Mullet Fingers shows him a beautiful spot by the creek. And Roy's father photocopies the file from Mother Paula's to show the absence of an Environmental Impact Report!

Think about the people and animals you've helped. Below, make a list of your good deeds, and then list those who have benefited from your help.

Now, think about those people and animals that have helped you. Make a list of their names and the ways in which they have enriched your life.

My Good Deeds	People and Animals I've Helped	People and Animals Who Have Helped Me	How They Have Enriched My Life

Any Questions?

When you finished reading *Hoot*, did you have questions that were left unanswered? Write a few of your questions on the back of this page.

Work in groups, or by yourself, to predict possible answers for all or some of the questions you wrote down, as well as those written below. When you have finished, share your predictions with the class.

1. Does Mullet Fingers ever return home to his mother? _____

2. Does Dana Matherson get locked up in juvenile hall? _____

3. What happens between Beatrice and her father? _____

   _____

4. Does Roy finally learn what his father's job is? _____

5. Does Mother Paula's build their pancake house in a new location?_____

   _____

6. What happens to the burrowing owls that Roy and his friends saved?_____

   _____

7. How does Dana Matherson treat Roy when he returns to school? _____

   _____

8. Does Roy ever see Mullet Fingers again?_____

9. Do Roy and Beatrice stay friends? _____

10. What happens to Kimberly Lou Dixon and her career? _____

    _____

11. What happens to Officer Delinko after he helps to save the owls? _____

    _____

12. Does Curly ever find a new job? _____

13. What type of career does Roy go into after he graduates? _____

14. Do Roy's parents decide to adopt Beatrice? _____

15. What happens to Mullet Fingers's mother? _____

16. Does another company in Florida try to build over owl burrows? If so, what happens?

    _____

Book Report Ideas

There are several ways to report on a book after you have read it. When you have finished *Hoot*, choose a method of reporting from the list below, or come up with your own idea on how best to report on this book.

Make a Book Jacket

Design a book jacket for this book. On the front, draw a picture that you feel best captures this story. On the back, write a paragraph or two which summarizes the main points of this book.

Make a Timeline

On paper, create a timeline to show the significant events in Roy's or Mullet Fingers's life. You may illustrate your timeline if you wish.

Design a Scrapbook

Use magazine pictures, photographs, and other illustrations to create a scrapbook that Roy might keep to document his life in Montana and then in Florida. He might choose to decorate his scrapbook with sketches of birds, trees, or adventures he's had in both states. He might paste photos of Beatrice and Mullet Fingers and the burrowing owls into his book.

Make a Collage

Using old magazines and photographs, design a collage that illustrates all of Roy's adventures in the novel.

Create a Time Capsule

What items might Roy put in a time capsule to remember how he and his friends fought Mother Paula's Pancake House and won? What container might he use as a time capsule?

Write a Biography

Do research to find out about the life of author Carl Hiaasen. You may use the Internet (Carl has his own website at http://www.carlhiaasen.com) or magazines. Write a biography, showing how Carl's experiences might have influenced *Hoot*.

Act Out a Play

With one or two other students, write a play featuring some of the characters in this novel. Then act out your play for your class.

Make Puppets

Using a variety of materials, design puppets to represent one or all of the characters in *Hoot*. You may decide to work with other students to write and perform a puppet show.

Research Ideas

As you read *Hoot*, you discovered geographical locations, events, and people about which you might wish to know more. To increase your understanding of the characters, places, and events in this novel, do research to find additional information.

Work alone or in groups to discover more about one or several of the items listed below. You may use books, magazines, encyclopedias, and the Internet to do research. Afterwards, share your findings with the class.

- Montana
- Florida
- the Everglades
- Audubon Society
- burrowing owls
- alligators
- cottonmouth moccasins
- homeless children
- Environmental Impact Plans
- raptors
- zoning laws
- environmental activism
- Seminole Indians
- law enforcement
- horror movies
- bullies
- development in Florida
- wildlife habitat
- The National Wildlife Federation
- boycotts
- first aid
- electrical storms
- bicycle theft
- guard dogs
- Newbery Award
- making commercials
- snowboarding
- skateboarding

Florida Festivities

In honor of *Hoot*, plan a Florida-themed celebration in your classroom. Consider inviting guests—another class, or your family members, to join your party.

Party Checklist

Three weeks before the party . . .

❏ Decide when and where the party will occur.

❏ Discuss how to work a Florida theme into your party. Will you dress in shorts and T-shirts, or in traditional Seminole attire? Perhaps you'll show videos of the Everglades and include a short Power Point presentation on Florida.

❏ Decide whether your class wants to invite guests to the party. If so, make and send invitations (page 39).

❏ Discuss decorations. You might want to display the papier-mâchè owls on page 11 and the Everglades diorama from page 26. Also think about how you could create trees and animals specific to Florida in your classroom. You might choose to show your commercials from page 27 at your party.

❏ Alternatively, you might choose to hold your party outside and around your new wildlife habitat from page 32.

Two weeks before the party . . .

❏ Decide what food/drink you will make as a class. This book provides a recipe for insect cookies on page 16 and owl-eye treats on page 40. What else might Roy and his friends like to eat and drink?

❏ Pass around a sign-up sheet. Each student should be encouraged to bring something unique to the party. They might bring food, sign up to play musical instruments, bring a favorite song or object for show and tell, or show off a skill such as skateboarding or bike riding.

❏ Send home a note to students' parents to let them know the day/date of the party, as well as what the student signed up to bring.

One week before the party . . .

❏ Send home a note reminding students of what they are to bring for the party.

❏ Buy and/or make decorations.

The day before the party . . .

❏ Make insect cookies and owl-eye treats.

The day of the party . . .

❏ Decorate the party space.

❏ Set up a DVD or video-player with your commercials.

Enjoy!

Florida Festivities *(cont.)*

Come to a PARTY!

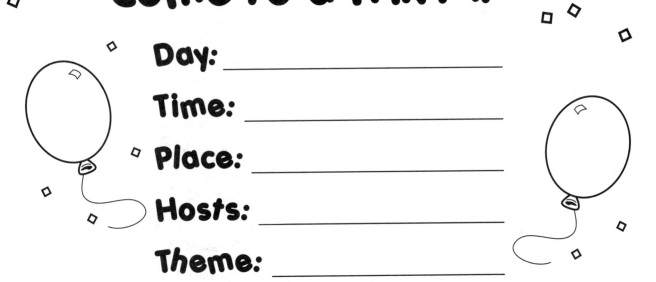

Day: _____

Time: _____

Place: _____

Hosts: _____

Theme: _____

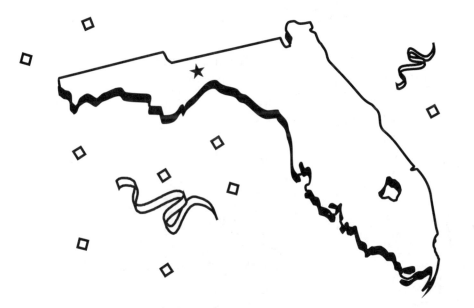

Owl-Eye Treats

Note to Teacher: Send home a written note with students, inquiring about pertinent food allergies, well in advance of preparing these treats.

Ingredients

- 1 package of chocolate kisses
- 1 package of M&Ms®
- 1 bag of candy corn
- 1 bag of pretzel twists
- parchment paper
- cookie sheet

Directions

1 • Preheat oven to 200° F (93°C). • Line cookie sheet with parchment paper. 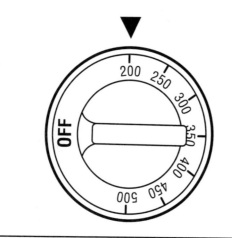	2 • Unwrap chocolate kisses. • Now, place pretzel twists on parchment paper. Put one chocolate kiss in each of the three holes in each pretzel, as shown below. 
3 • Place cookie sheet in oven and bake treats for approximately three and a half minutes. • Remove cookie sheet and immediately place one M&M® candy in the center of each of the two upper melted chocolate kisses for eyes, as shown below. Flatten slightly. 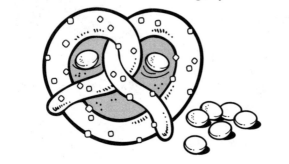	4 • Place one candy corn on the lower melted chocolate kiss for a beak, as shown below. • Let treats cool, and then eat. Makes 16 servings. 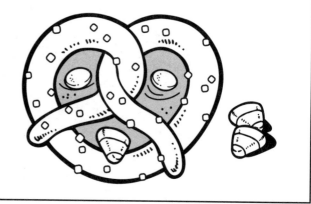

Raptor Rehabilitation Centers

All around the world, people work to nurse injured owls, eagles, hawks, falcons, osprey, and kites back to health. In some cases, these raptor rehabilitation centers are open to the public for tours.

Using your knowledge of how to write a business letter from page 23, write or e-mail one or more of the raptor centers from the list below. Then request literature for more information on the important work being done to protect raptors such as the burrowing owls in Florida.

To find raptor centers in your area, type the words "Raptor Center" into an Internet search engine.

The Avian Reconditioning Center

http://www.arc4raptors.org
323 West Lester Road
Apopka, Florida 32712
info@adoptabird.org
Offers membership, educational programs, web cams, and
adopt-a-bird programs.

Cascades Raptor Center

http://www.eraptors.org
P.O. Box 5386
Eugene, Oregon 97405
info@eraptors.org
Offers membership, educational programs, videos on website, and adopt-a-raptor programs.

Alaska Raptor Center

http://www.alaskaraptor.org
1000 Raptor Way
Sitka, Alaska 99835
director.alaskaraptor@alaska.com
Offers membership, educational programs, and
adopt-a-raptor programs.

Illinois Raptor Center

http://www.illinoisraptorcenter.org
5695 West Hill Road
Decatur, Illinois 62522
illinoisraptorcenter@insightbb.com
Offers membership, educational programs, and informational brochures.

Hudson Valley Raptor Center

http://www.hvraptors.com
148 South Road
Stanfordville, New York 12581
Donatracy@hotmail.com
Offers membership, educational programs, videos on website, and adopt-a-raptor programs.

Field Trips and Class Visits

Now that your students have learned all about raptor conservation and other environmental concerns, they may enjoy taking one or more field trips to related areas, or inviting in a guest speaker.

Choose an activity from the list below and locate the appropriate contact person in the phone book or on the Internet. Be sure to call at least two weeks in advance, to give the staff plenty of time to prepare for the event.

A Local Raptor or Wildlife Rehabilitation Center

See the list on the previous page for ideas, or consult the phone book and/or the Internet for wildlife rehabilitators in your area. Students may opt to visit a facility, or invite directors and/or volunteers for a class visit.

Falconers

Falconry is a sport which involves using a raptor to hunt live prey. Students may enjoy a visit from a professional falconer and his/her bird, or a trip out to the field to watch the couple at work.

City Zoo

Often, the local zoo presents wild raptors in a natural setting. Some zoos incorporate trained raptors in exciting wildlife presentations. In addition, raptor trainers may be willing to visit your classroom with their birds.

City Planners

After reading *Hoot*, students may be curious about zoning laws and the balance of new construction in their city with wildlife conservation. A local city planner can answer questions and address concerns.

Environmentally-Friendly Construction Companies

More and more, construction companies that bill themselves as environmentally friendly build houses and other buildings with an eye for preserving natural habitat and using recycled materials. Consider taking a tour of one of their construction sites, or inviting a representative into your classroom to answer questions.

Florida Native

If you aren't located in Florida, why not send a note home with students to ask if parents or grandparents are originally from Florida. Guest speakers can bring in photographs, videos, and stories that will illuminate life in Florida, and Roy's experiences in his new state, for your students.

Objective Test and Essay

Matching: Write the letter of the correct description next to each character.

_____ 1. Roy Eberhardt

a. He's a bully who likes to beat up weaker kids.

_____ 2. Beatrice

b. She points out that sometimes there's a conflict between one's head and heart.

_____ 3. Mullet Fingers

c. He discovered alligators in his port-a-potties.

_____ 4. Mr. Eberhardt

d. They live on the construction site where Mother Paula's Pancake House will be built.

_____ 5. Curly

e. In Florida, he learns to stand up for injustice even though he's still a kid.

_____ 6. Officer Delinko

f. She's an actress and a member of the Audubon Society.

_____ 7. Dana Matherson

g. He discovers that there is no Environmental Impact Statement for the Mother Paula's construction site.

_____ 8. Kimberly Lou Dixon

h. He's a runaway with creative methods of solving problems.

_____ 9. Mrs. Eberhardt

i. She's a tough girl with a beautiful singing voice.

_____ 10. burrowing owls

j. He is dismayed when someone paints the windows of his car black.

True or False: Answer true or false in the blanks below.

_____ 1. At the end of the book, Roy still dislikes Florida and can't wait to move back to Montana.

_____ 2. Beatrice and Mullet Fingers have a loving family.

_____ 3. Mr. Eberhardt helps Roy to stop construction on Mother Paula's Pancake House.

_____ 4. Officer Delinko gets fired from his job for saving owls.

_____ 5. Kimberly Lou Dixon loves birds and doesn't want to put the owls in danger.

Short Answer: Write a brief response on separate paper.

1. Why does Roy decide to help in the fight to save the burrowing owls?

2. Why does Chuck Muckle try to pretend that the burrowing owls aren't living on the construction site?

3. Why does Beatrice decide to protect Roy?

4. How does Dana Matherson get what he deserves by the end of the novel?

Essay: Respond to the following on separate paper.

Roy and Mullet Fingers are both environmental activists—that is, they both take action to protect the habitat of burrowing owls. However, each boy has a unique approach to activism. How are these approaches different? How are they the same?

Responding to Quotes

On a separate piece of paper, respond to the following quotes as selected by your teacher.

Chapter One: "Roy was sure that the barefoot boy would catch all kinds of grief from Dana and the other big kids once he boarded the bus, but that didn't happen . . . ."

Chapter Four: "Vandalism and trespassing weren't big-time crimes, but Officer Delinko was intrigued by the continuing pattern of mischief at the future site of Mother Paula's All-American Pancake House."

Chapter Six: "There was Beatrice Leep, sitting on his bicycle. She said, 'What's in the shoebox, cowgirl?'"

Chapter Nine: "The dog trainer then had hauled him toward the fence to point out another moccasin, then another, and still another—nine in all."

Chapter Ten: "Mullet Fingers peeled off the plastic wrapper and scooped out a handful of ground beef, which he carefully rolled into six perfect little meatballs."

Chapter Eleven: "'The emergency room!' she cried breathlessly. 'Roy's been hurt!'"

Chapter Thirteen: "'Dad, he's really not a bad kid,' Roy said when he finished. 'All he's trying to do is save the owls.'"

Chapter Fifteen: "'I know where there's a whole case of cigarettes. If you promise not to beat me up, I'll show you.'"

Chapter Sixteen: "Roy had always thought that Beatrice Leep wasn't afraid of anything, but she didn't look so fearless now . . . . it was hard to imagine living in a house where the grownups behaved so idiotically."

Chapter Sixteen: "In a snit, Curly stomped toward the third and last piece of equipment, a grader. Again, no driver's seat."

Chapter Eighteen: "It was a baby owl, no more than five or six inches tall. Officer Delinko had never seen anything so delicately perfect."

Chapter Twenty: "'What in the world'd you say to those kids yesterday?' Beatrice asked. 'You promise them free flapjacks or something?'"

Chapter Twenty-One: "Roy opened the folder and broke into a grin. 'This is the file from City Hall, isn't it?'"

Epilogue: "He lifted the soggy sneaker and peeked inside. There he spied a mullet no larger than a man's index finger, flipping and splashing to protest its captivity."

Conversations

Work in groups according to the numbers in parentheses to write or act out the conversations that might have occurred in each of the following situations in *Hoot*.

- Roy tells the bus driver that Dana Matherson beat him up. (2 people)

- Mullet Fingers tells Beatrice what he did to Officer Delinko's patrol car. (2 people)

- Beatrice and her friends discuss Roy over lunch in the school cafeteria. (3–4 people)

- Mullet Fingers tells Beatrice to find Roy after he's been bitten by a dog. (2 people)

- Garrett and his friends talk about the conflict between Roy and Dana. (3–4 people)

- Roy's parents talk about their son and how he's trying to save the burrowing owls. (2 people)

- Lonna kicks Mullet Fingers out of her house and forces him to go to a boarding school. (2 people)

- Curly calls his mother and tells her about the trouble he's been having at Mother Paula's construction site. (2 people)

- Chuck Muckle talks to his best friend about the letter that Beatrice and Mullet Fingers wrote to him. (2 people)

- Mullet Fingers tells Beatrice why he believes saving the burrowing owls is so important. (2 people)

- Roy's parents talk about how Lonna doesn't want Mullet Fingers. (2 people)

- Lonna and Beatrice's father argue with Mullet Fingers and Beatrice. (4 people)

- Kimberly Lou Dixon tells a newspaper reporter why she quit being Mother Paula in commercials for the Pancake House. (2 people)

- Mr. Ryan talks with Miss Hennepin about Roy. (2 people)

- Roy's parents talk about the missing permit in the Mother Paula's file. (2 people)

- The burrowing owls talk among themselves about what is happening to their land. (3–4 people)

- Officer Delinko tells his supervisor why he lied in order to protect the burrowing owls. (2 people)

- Beatrice, Roy, and Mullet Fingers meet at the creek to discuss life after saving the burrowing owls. (3 people)

Bibliography of Related Reading

Fiction

Bloor, Edward. *Tangerine*. Harcourt, 1997.

Creech, Sharon. *Walk Two Moons*. Harper Collins, 1994.

DiCamillo, Kate. *Because of Winn-Dixie*. Candlewick, 2000.

George, Jean Craighead. *Frightful's Mountain*. Puffin, 2001.

Hiaasen, Carl. *Flush*. Knopf, 2005.

Lasky, Kathryn. *Guardians of Ga'hoole* series. Scholastic, 2005.

London, Jack. *Call of the Wild*. Meadowbook, 1999.

Mowat, Farley. *Owls in the Family*. Yearling, 1996.

Rawlings, Marjorie Kinnan. *The Yearling*. Atheneum, 1985.

Sachar, Louis. *Holes*. Yearling, 2000.

Smith, Roland. *Jaguar*. Hyperion, 1998.

Nonfiction

Duncan, James R. *Owls of the World: Their Lives, Behavior, and Survival*. Firefly, 2003.

Hammerslough, Jane. *Owl Puke: Book and Owl Pellet*. Workman, 2003.

Sattler, Helen Roney. *The Book of North American Owls*. Clarion, 1998.

Sutton, Patricia Taylor. *How to Spot an Owl*. Houghton Mifflin, 1999.

Williams, Winston. *Florida's Fabulous Birds*. World Publications, 1986.

Williams, Winston and Tim Ohr. *Florida's Fabulous Places*. World Publications, 1998.

Websites

http://www.owlpages.com (type in burrowing owl)

http://www.birds.cornell.edu/programs/AllAboutBirds/BirdGuide (type in burrowing owl)

http://members.aol.com/pjbowen/owls.html (information about the Florida burrowing owl project)

http://www.floridanature.org (information about Florida flora and fauna)

Answer Key

Page 10

1. Roy is interested in the strange boy outside the bus window because the boy is running, he doesn't have any shoes, and he doesn't appear to be going to school.
2. Roy doesn't have a hometown because his family moves frequently, and just moved to Florida from Montana.
3. Miss Hennepin suspends Roy from the bus because he punched Dana Matherson.
4. Mr. Eberhardt is angry when he finds out about Roy's fight with Dana. He thinks it's unfair that Roy was punished when Dana had started the fight.
5. Officer Delinko thinks that someone put alligators in the toilets as revenge against Mother Paula's Pancake House.
6. Officer Delinko wants to solve the mystery of the vandalism at the construction site because he likes to solve crimes and hopes for a promotion.
7. Beatrice is surprised when Roy talks to her in the cafeteria because she thought that she had intimidated him.
8. Roy finds the remains of a campfire, as well as garbage, clothes, and footprints in the thicket near the golf course.

Page 13

1. Florida became part of the United States on March 3, 1845.
2. Florida is 170,451 square kilometers, or 58,560 square miles.

3–6: Answers will vary

3. Three types of native animals that live in Florida are the Florida panther, the black bear, and the manatee.
4. Three types of native reptiles that live in Florida are the American alligator, the Florida snapping turtle, and the Florida water snake.
5. Three types of native birds that live in Florida are the mockingbird, kestrel, and the hummingbird.
6. The Everglades are wetlands. They are home to alligators and crocodiles. Numerous types of birds, and mangrove and cypress swamps are in Florida.
7. Florida's state bird is the mockingbird.
8. Florida's state tree is the sabal palm.
9. Florida's state flower is the orange blossom.
10. The ocean that surrounds Florida is the Atlantic.

Page 15

1. Officer Delinko has to go on desk duty because he slept through surveillance duty while delinquents painted the windows of his patrol car.
2. Beatrice takes Roy's bike so that she can get to Mullet Fingers quickly. She is also suspicious because Roy is trying to find her brother.
3. Beatrice bites a hole in Roy's bike tire so he'll have an excuse for being late when he gets home.
4. Roy is allowed back on the school bus because his mother told Miss Hennepin it was unfair to punish him if Dana wasn't going to be punished.
5. Roy lets Dana hit him on the school bus because he doesn't want to cower and beg, and he also wants Dana to get the bullying out of his system.
6. Roy tries not to worry his parents because his mother had lost her second baby, and he was an only child.
7. Kalo takes his dogs away from the construction site because someone has let loose poisonous snakes.
8. Curly is in trouble with Chuck Muckle because the construction of Mother Paula's Pancake House has been delayed after snakes were set loose on the property.

Page 20

1. Beatrice punishes Dana for attacking Roy in the closet by stripping him down to his underpants and tying him to a flagpole.
2. Lonna doesn't try to find her son because they don't get along and she is "fed up" with him.
3. Mullet Fingers gets bitten when he lets snakes loose on the construction site and a dog bites him.
4. Roy gives the emergency room clerk his own name instead of that of Mullet Fingers because he wants to get the boy into a hospital bed quickly, and Mullet doesn't want Lonna to be notified.
5. Mullet Fingers is concerned about the burrowing owls because they will lose their homes if Mother Paula's Pancake House is constructed on the site.
6. Roy goes to see Dana Matherson hoping that they can work things out so that he can be free to solve the problems involving Mullet Fingers and the owls.
7. When Chuck E. Muckle received Beatrice's letter, he wrote a letter to her stating his concern for the environment, and assured her that all necessary permits would be obtained.
8. Mullet Fingers takes Roy to the creek and shows him an old boat called the Molly Bell. He also shows him how he can catch a fish barehanded.

Page 25

1. Roy tells Dana about a carton of cigarettes in the construction trailer so that Curly will think Dana has been committing vandalism on the construction site. He hopes Dana will go to jail.
2. The police may lock Dana up in juvenile hall because he already had a record, and because vandalism is illegal.
3. Someone removed the seats on the construction equipment at the Mother Paula's site so that construction on the Pancake House would be delayed.

Answer Key (cont.)

4. On the airboat trip through the Everglades, Roy discovers that Florida is just as wild as Montana.
5. Beatrice breaks into Roy's house because her parents are fighting, and she needs somewhere safe to sleep.
6. Chuck Muckle asks Curly to say that the owl burrows are deserted because it is illegal to build over their homes, and he has not obtained an Environmental Impact Statement.
7. When Officer Delinko gives Dana a plastic alligator, he discovers that Dana is afraid of alligators.
8. This answer is subjective. Students may guess that Chuck E. Muckle checked out the file and hid it. Accept all reasonable answers.

Page 28

1. The Seminole nation came into existence roughly around the late 1700s. Euchee, Yamasee, Timugua, Tequesta, Abalachi, Coça, and Creek tribes made up this nation.
2. The United States government wanted to remove the Seminole Indians from Florida because they wanted to claim the territory as their own.
3. Seminole leader Osceola was a warrior, and he is famous because he protested the Indian Removal Act. He witnessed many battles between Seminoles and the U.S. government.
4. The Seminoles call themselves "The Unconquered People" because after the second Seminole war, the U.S. government gave up trying to remove the tribe from their land.
5. The Seminoles produce painting, basketry, dolls, and beadwork.
6. The Seminole tribe maintains six reservations in Florida. They are Big Cypress, Tampa, Hollywood, Brighton, Immokalee and Fort Pierce.
7. The Seminoles speak Muscogee and Miccosukee, aside from English.

8. Seminole patchwork is blocks or bars of alternating color, often in a sawtooth design. These bands are sewn directly into a garment.
9. The Seminole "Chickee" is a thatched hut—palmetto fronds over a wooden frame.

Page 30

1. Officer Delinko discovers the burrowing owls living on the construction site and feels sad that their homes may be destroyed. He thinks they are perfect little birds.
2. Roy borrows his mother's camera to prove to authorities that owls live on the construction site.
3. Mullet Fingers pushes Roy out of the truck because he says he's caused Roy enough trouble, and it's his "war" now. He thinks it's time to play hardball.
4. Roy's report in class is related to "Current Events" because the next day, construction will destroy the burrowing owls' habitat.
5. When she learns about the owls, Kimberly Lou Dixon says she loves birds. She shows her Audubon card and quits being Mother Paula in commercials.
6. Officer Delinko doesn't tell Chuck Muckle that Mullet Fingers' snakes are only rubber because he wants to help save the owls.
7. The missing Environmental Impact Statement is so important in the case against Mother Paula's because burrowing owls are a protected species and Mother Paula's knows that if they are found on the construction site, no building will occur.
8. The answer to this question is subjective. Roy suspects that Mullet Fingers is living near the creek. Accept all reasonable answers.

Page 43

Matching

1. e		6. j	
2. i		7. a	
3. h		8. f	
4. g		9. b	
5. c		10. d	

True or False

1. F
2. F
3. T
4. F
5. T

Short Answer

1. Roy realizes that without his help, the owls will lose their homes. He wants to help Beatrice and Mullet Fingers fight injustice.
2. Chuck Muckle tries to pretend that the burrowing owls aren't living on the construction site so that he can go ahead and bulldoze over their homes.
3. Beatrice decides to protect Roy because he brings shoes to her brother and seems genuinely concerned about him, and about the owls. Also, she admires him for standing up to Dana Matherson.
4. Dana Matherson is recaptured after trying to escape juvenile hall, and he can no longer bully other kids.

Essay

Answers will vary. Accept reasonable and well-supported answers.

Page 44

Grade students on comprehension of the story as evidenced by the length of answers and depth of responses.

Page 45

Grade students on comprehension of the story, knowledge of the characters, and creativity.